Where Are the Altars?

Where Are the Altars?

Joy Mead

WILD GOOSE PUBLICATIONS
www.ionabooks.com

Published by
Wild Goose Publications
Fourth Floor, Savoy House, 140 Sauchiehall Street, Glasgow G2 3DH, UK,
the publishing division of the Iona Community.
Scottish Charity No. SCO03794.
Limited Company Reg. No. SCO96243.

ISBN 978-1-905010-36-3

Cover painting © Sophie Hacker
Cover design © 2007 Wild Goose Publications

Overseas distribution:
N. America: Novalis/Bayard, 10 Lower Spadina Ave., Suite 400, Toronto, Ontario M5V 2Z
Australia: Willow Connection Pty Ltd, Unit 4A, 3-9 Kenneth Road, Manly Vale, NSW 2093
New Zealand: Pleroma Christian Supplies, Higginson St., Otane 4170, Central Hawkes Bay

Printed by Thomson Litho, East Kilbride, Scotland

Contents

Part Two: Circles, bowls and thresholds

Part Three: Because of love

Part Four : A soaring vision

An Afterthought: The seven colours of imagination

Notes and acknowledgements   154

Has this been always so?
Have we been ever seeking
in sacred place
and lifeless ritual
the birthing of our nature;
wanting The One Truth
and missing many truths?

And is the secret of our becoming
going into the emptiness
where what might have been
and what has been:
suffering and weeping
rejoicing and singing
are truly one.

Who are the priests?
Where are the altars?
These are questions
which have no answers
but a passion to belong
and the movement
of an empty cross
into a bigger area
of redemption.

I look into the brief existence
of a flower with certainty
of nothing but that its fragility
is the colour of eternity.

Introduction

Most of the poems and pieces in this collection are new, one or two have appeared in other places. There is a mixture of styles, from the more meditative to my modest attempt at the non-literary approach of the French poet Jacques Prévert ('At the hospital', 'The end of summer' and 'Soapbox').

Poetry is about showing not telling. You'll find no definitive answer to the question in the book's title. I have tried in all the poems and pieces in this book to show my understanding of a way of life that is incarnational, a spirituality that engages with people, things and the joys and sorrows of daily life.

The story of the first Pentecost is a vision of spirituality that is a healing of our world not a leap into other worlds. Whichever way we look at its symbolism the story is about a mind-blowing, heart-searching moment but it isn't a once-and-for-all happening. It's ongoing and energising hope here, now, in this world, in this place. Look carefully at when and where the story in Acts is set – not exactly a place set apart – more like the motorway services I tell of in Part One. Definitely a social context.

This book is something, perhaps only a beginning or small part, of how all this works in terms of day-to-day ordinary living. It's about seeing the many stories that are part of the one story, recognising the connections that make us whole human beings. When strangers share stories, when someone lays a hand on your arm and holds your attention – like Coleridge's ancient mariner – that's a quiet resurrection moment when you see into the heart of things and trust in life. Perhaps you lose your soul when you can't tell a story about something that happens to you.

I like to think that there is a link here with painters and poets and all people trying to find their own words and images for their experiences, to express what it means to be fully human. This is about the beauty of language, how we use it in order to be truly engaged with life in all its wonder and fragility, to express the complexity of human emotions, to gather light, to write a rainbow …

Joy Mead, Spring 2007

Part One:

Small Things and Given Moments

Introduction

Motorway services are not among my favourite places – and not places where I'd naturally think about spirituality.

But as I stood in the queue waiting for coffee I became conscious of the woman beside me. She was looking anxiously over her shoulder towards an older woman at a table nearby. We began a conversation. She told me her story. The older woman waiting for a cup of tea was her mother, who had Alzheimer's. Her mother who could still enjoy the small pleasure of a good cup of tea, and the remaining memories it prompted. The common is sanctified in small acts of care and kindness, in knowing how to enjoy the given moments in any day.

Engagement came through story and tea: a moment of contact, of meeting, of connection. Not what you'd necessarily call a spiritual or poetic moment or recognise as such, but it was! I heard her story and we exchanged the ordinary language of ordinary people: things for today, stories for tomorrow. Things not abstractions. The poetry is in the things. Anton Chekhov once said to a student attempting to write about a tricky abstraction: beauty: 'Cut out all those pages about beautiful moonlight. Show us the moon's reflection in a piece of broken glass.'

I was interested to read of a study by Daniel Everett into the language of the Pirahã people of the Brazilian Amazon. 'Some of the brightest, pleasantest, most loving people I know,' he says. Their culture constrains communication to non-abstract subjects which fall within the immediate experience of the speaker.

I find myself bombarded with annunciations: sunlight on dead leaves, the patterns of tree bark, daisies and dandelion seeds, bread, flowers, shoes, butterflies, the smile of a child, a baby's hands, an old woman's lined face, pictures of the Sri Lankan children going back to school after the tsunami ...... the tears of a stranger ... Things, events, people – bathed in a special light – amazing me with their wonder, mystery and value, part of a world more extraordinary than I can take in. (Isn't this what a visit from an angel is?) It's pure poetry: a way of seeing the world as well as a way of writing about it. The rarest and purest generosity is giving our full attention to the feel, the smell, the look, the sound of things themselves, to the presence of a man, woman or child. What we see depends not only on the source of light but on our awareness, our imaginative capacity to receive the light. Imagination – earthed and grounded in our own experience – matters. It has a profound physical effect on all we are and do.

When George MacLeod, founder of the Iona Community, spoke of 'every blessed thing' he meant just that. There is no thing, no particular, untouched by the spirit. All is seen and valued within the wonder of the whole.

Things

In this room
I breathe words.
Things with one another
make a story:

books on ledge and shelf
on desk and floor
… books on books,
a 'book chair' I never use,
poems on postcards,
an invitation to an authors' party –
I can't go;

a medieval allegory of the scribe's tools
to remind me of the responsibility of words;

photographs of William, Alasdair,
Emily and Oliver –
to remind me of tomorrow;

a key from a piano
that once made music
in Iona Abbey,
stones from St Columba's Bay
that still shout aloud;

a framed strawberry,
a large cut-out Tigger,
a sparkly apple,
paper flowers from a 'Blooming Women Day' –
long ago in Manchester,

a bunch of cut-out cardboard cornflowers
from Catherine and Andrew's wedding day;

a silver spoon from Glasgow University,
a cross from Peru,
peace poppies on a string,
a waving ladybird clock –
Catherine says, 'Every home should have one' –
a papier-mâché penguin
the children next door made for me,
a 'Mouseman' book rack;

a dream catcher – complete with invisible dreams,
the 'Growing hope' collage Jan made for me
in 1995 – the year I had cancer,
the empty John Leach bowl Ian gave me
which fits perfectly in my open hands.

Learning to paint a walnut

I am looking at a walnut,
attending to the wrinkles
of its wood-brown body
which holds, unseen,
two crumpled seed-leaves.

For a fleeting moment
I might imagine the walnut
as shell halves, full of sunlight,
making toy boats for a child

or see the walnut tree
where a boy swings
on his first birthday.

Brush and colour suggest
that I look only at what is here

while they remind me
that this imagining,
this taking care,
is open enough
to be called prayer.

Shoes *

A midden of worn shoes in a hut,
800,000 pairs: the absurdity
of so many caged shoes.

I'm tempted to zoom in,
brush off the dust of death,
feel each scuff and crease,
sense each pinch and pressure,

to try on Sabbath best shoes,
the ones to wear when going
on a journey,
touch a small boy's shoe
and feel the shape of running feet,
hopping pavements, avoiding cracks,
brush my hands over
the crumpled wisdom
of well-worked boots,

to try to find the missing faces –
the men, women and children –
in this collective story.

How personal shoes are.
And how impossible
to walk in someone else's shoes.

* At Majdanek, two miles from Lublin, Poland, site of a Nazi death camp. At the Majdanek
Memorial Museum there is a memorial containing the ashes of around 100,000 Holocaust
victims, and an exhibit of the 800,000 pairs of shoes that were found at Majdanek when the
camp was liberated, on July 23, 1944. See www.nizkor.org

Speaking peace

(Fionnphort 2002)

There are stories in the wind today.
I breathe the language of a field
heady with the scent of midsummer
meadowsweet: favourite flower
to honey the mead,
strew rooms with sweetness
that makes hearts glad.
Cuchulainn*, long ago hero,
rode out, we are told,
with the creamy blossoms
in his belt to cool his rage.

And exuberant loosestrife,
which patterns the same meadow
with ripples the colour
of purple-red passion,
once calmed ox and horse
yoked together.

Legendary Irish hero whose violent story is told in The Ulster Cycle

The Christmas star

We should take it down
but it hangs
long after the celebrations
have been forgotten:
  a memory of the cradle,
  a memorial
  for the frightened children.

And William knows
that Grandma and Granddad
will always have a star
shining in the dark
over the last stair

before his feet
touch the ground.

Being human

I can't imagine wholeness
without the intense green
of a single blade of grass,
the way light plays
on the underside
of hornbeam leaves,

the purple of heather-covered hills,
the unreachable blue
of a carpet of bluebells
and their scent
that is childhood,

the morning yellow promise
of a primrose,
the flash of red
of a woodpecker's head,

the way water runs
over sand on the shore
leaving ripple patterns
I know won't last,

the sound of sea
sucking on stones
and the river running
over rocks,

the slant of winter sun
colouring dormant trees,

one white flower in a field
of shadows

and your voice saying
my name.

Well-being

There is blessing
in things that matter, together:

the quiver of joy each year
when the first daffodil opens,
the way a sightless dying man touches
a young girl's engagement ring –
and remembers his long-dead love,
Iona dawn – the light
on my face – and knowing
this is the place to be,
looking into the faces
of friends
in a crowded teashop,
the way cotton grass
catches both wind and sun,
daisies and dandelions that come
from nowhere,
stillness held in an empty bowl
and the hands around it,
a child who puts a hand
in mine telling me
there is tomorrow,
the spring blossom,
bee-filled, tongue-tingling promise
of an apple,

an elderly Sikh
early one morning in High Wycombe
carrying a sheaf of gladioli,
fragile threads of chance
that make encounters
into friendships,
the barely perceptible
and never-to-be-held moment
when the eyes that see
and the wild rose that is seen
are one.

Paperweight

My fingers close
around a dandelion clock
out of time
in a ball of glass.

And I see
how things could be:
a haze of floating seeds
filling the early summer air
with kisses and promises,
a fragile potential
to scatter the sites of our folly
with outbursts of pure gold.

Every thing

Holiness: the way light defines
beyond itself,
links my being with what I see:
flowers and distant mountains,
the sea and the salt
of the sea,
softer, more ambiguous forms,
half visible, remembered or suspected.

Many lives, many things
in one light.
All seeing is true:
human eyes, butterfly eyes,
bird eyes, bee eyes.

Thoughts rest fleetingly
on the way the light
reveals things.

Grass snake

Olive-grey coil
of stillness, head up
orange collar
catching the sun,
watching

becomes
in a moment
all movement,
flowing like warm oil
into the grass.

The wonder could be
it comes so close
to where we sit

and yet I think
the wonder
is to look at it.

Tonight there may be stars
here in the same way
as the snake is here
and has always known
something.

Empty shoes

A pair of gold strappy sandals,
worn down by dancing and treading lightly
on daisied lawns at dawn,
disturbed in the dust
of an old woman's wardrobe;
one baby shoe tied to the fence
of an army base;
dirty trainers in a teenager's bedroom;
one boot washed up on a river bank;
shoes left at the door of a mosque;
the shoes Daley Thompson
took from the feet of Kelly Holmes
after she won the Olympic gold;
the sandals by the sea that remind me
of school corridors
and endless summertime.

Unworn shoes float away in a flood;
shoes of bomb victims
lie scattered in a road;
rows of unneeded shoes wait
in the wardrobes of the powerful
after their downfall;
shoes fill a tree in a park*
with stories – like souls after death –
hanging unclaimed.

Shoes, telling of holy ground
they once walked on.

* Tree dressing is an ancient tradition expressing the value of trees. Most often trees are
decorated during harvest or at midwinter solstice to give thanks for abundance or the
promise of spring, but the tradition has been adapted in many communities around the
world to celebrate or mark other significant events or concerns.

Living in the cracks

Ivy-leaved Toadflax
… a name that gives nothing
away – almost a disguise

to cover the tales
other names tell:
Travelling Sailor
(come a long journey)
Mother of Thousands
(giving birth to stories)
Madonna's Flower
(looking to the angels).

Seeds came in secretly
centuries ago, hidden in the cracks
of marble figures from Italy.

Migrant, refugee, stranger –
not knowing how to go wild
with the yellow Common Toadflax
that dances in waste places –
you developed a liking for domestic walls,
embedded yourself in Cotswold stone
and became the Oxford Weed.

Then when the time was right,
your offspring travelled secretly

to the edges,

to the walls of the Abbey
on Iona where a cascade of flowers
touches my bare legs
like the hands of forgotten children

or to become, on Yeats's tower,
like poetry: a conversation
that connects, an interruption,
tentative maybe, but big enough

to fill the cracks of our domesticity
and colour our broken places.
Part of the scene; here to stay.

Ancient foliot turret-clock

(At Hadden Hall, Bakewell, Derbyshire)

The unworking parts
of the clock we watched
are a mocking reminder
of our foolish attempts
to measure straight
and true, the journey
from here to tomorrow.

The clock has stopped –
its question hangs in the air.

Beyond this room
a field of dandelion clocks
knows its own time
remarkably well.

A day for making memories

A blackbird singing
on an empty day
calls across time and space,
through fragments of despair
and the shadows of lost dreams.

The air holds his haunting melody
of hope, the promise of joy
beyond laughter, deeper
than my tears.

Wool-gathering

(May 2006)

On Exmoor this year
they tell of the way
whole fleeces fall from sheep,
blind ewes walk away
from their lambs

and the weather deals strange destruction.

These stories wrap themselves around
my memories of another time out of joint.

Knitted-up wartime wool
was unravelled and remade
into a jumper and skirt
I'm wearing as a child
in a black-and-white photograph.
Mum wears her green dress,
clips like gold leaves at the neck.

Dad, home from the war,
made a wool-winder –
like a deformed spinning wheel
in an untold fairy tale.
It became the centre
of a story
some force prevents
me from unwinding.

I wonder at the fleece
that falls unseen
from the sheep
on the moor,
its power to protect
the innocent, abandoned.
It weighs no more
than the childhood I carry
in my arms.

April, 2006

(For Fred, with love)

April, Eliot's cruellest month*:
the air heady with promise.

Beech leaves unfurl
and the blue
of bluebells is the deepest
of mysteries in the quiet
of the moment.

Frail things that live
and once lived,
yesterdays lost in the mist,
tomorrows that may not be,
gather in a dreamlike web.

So I think of you, dear friend,
and cells that die
taking with them
words that shape
images of the past
and pictures of the future.

What is now beyond telling
is written on your skin,
hidden deep in your eyes,
carried on every hair of your head.

You gather light
sufficient for today

like the flowers I saw once
locked in a cage
early in the morning
on a railway platform.

See T.S. Eliot's The Waste Land

Marmalade

Oranges, the Chinese tell us,
bring good fortune
and I have hope
for these, an unexpected gift,
lifting my mood,
filling the room
with gathered light.

They are washed and ready.
Our pith-paring knives
cut, chop and release
their fragrant juices
into the waiting pan.

They only pretend to be sweet.
So we measure a mountain of sugar.
Then add a lemon for extra sharpness –
for this is an ambiguous process –
and collect, for the setting,
hundreds of lost possibilities
in a muslin squeeze
of pips and pith.

Three hours
and many licked spoons later
a bitter-sweetness flows
into jars that glow
like amber lanterns.

Ratatouille*

I'm cutting up the colour
of the warm south –
peppers, onions, tomatoes, courgettes
(in Nice they say no aubergines) –
to make a farmer's dish
of summer vegetables.

This is food, bright and whole
never mushy,
each vegetable loving itself
separate yet not distant.

It tastes like a rainbow
smells like sunlight
on a summer afternoon

and looks like friendship.

Meaning 'to toss food'

Philip said, 'Come and see'

(John 1:46)

In an ordinary shed – a little house you call it –
seven dwarfs gather behind bags of compost:
like the essence of a fairy story
lost in literalism. A child's delight
raises garden gnomes
to the place of angels.

And we can laugh together
and know that the facts of the world
are not the end of the story.

Waitrose in December:
Christmas trees and piped carols.
You see it first: a rainbow
in the darkening sky,
outshining the vanity
of tinsel and fairy lights.

The roar of the jet overhead
drowns out birdsong
and children's voices
but you hear a grasshopper
beside the path. We find it
in the long grass and delight
in its immense littleness.

At the edge of a wood
in the heat of the afternoon:
the sound of a blackbird,
the movement of squirrels,
the brief sight of the owl
as it flies across our path
in daytime: wanting to be seen
and the boy
for whom time has no edges,
looking for blackberries in June.

An enigmatic invitation
disturbs our personal peace,
leads us out from under our fig trees
to see the whole world
in the shape of a story
that is always
just beginning:

Come and see.

Iona stones

At this bright edge
light plays on stones
and wind overlays them
like a fine cloth.

I can feel their secrets,
the way they hold
colours, not passive
but still … waiting.
Stones will be here
at the end.

There is it seems
some connection
between an old woman resting
against the Abbey wall
and a stone being warmed
by the sun.

Kissing crusts

Not the way they meet
secretly, in the heat
of the moment

but the way they break
apart – an almost violent
shock, revealing
their beginnings,
letting out the smell
of secrets, fear
of exposure,
the warm deeps,
the insides of things
we might think
best kept hidden.

To make a poem

learn to swim without water,
or fly on the ground:
it's all make-believe.

Walk on water:
not an element for walking
unless you trust
imagination.

Walk on air – sometimes.
Say 'Yes' to the moment.

But the hard task
will always be
to walk lightly
on your own element:
the good earth.

To my newborn grandson

I want to say
that being human
is as much about poetry
as faith, as much about feet
as soul.

The moments when I see
into the heart of things
have little to do with beliefs
or creeds … churches, altars
or black-robed priests.
And everything to do with

a story I tell
about the surprises
of ordinary days.

Everything to do
with the brush of daisy petals
against my bare feet,
and the feel of life
in the bread as it rises
in my hands.

Everything to do with the surprise
of love in newborn eyes
staring back at me
from the depths of a self
you will not find
but create as you live
remembering not the moment
of your birth but the wonder
of your life.

Part Two:

Circles, Bowls and Thresholds

Introduction

In one of his best-known prayers, George MacLeod says:

… all things consist and hang together:
The very atom is light energy,
The grass is vibrant,
The rocks pulsate.

All is in flux; turn but a stone and an angel moves …

I like that! God, verb not noun, for me has to be the surprising processes of the world of which we're part: shorthand for astonishing and complex, yet ordinary and everyday happenings: eating, drinking, gardening, lovemaking …… God is what connects us with all things, makes us wholly human.

We might remember that the sand Jesus wrote in with his finger in the story (John 8:1–11) was *particular* sand in a *particular* place within a story for all time.

Our lives are lived in time – not a line we walk but a consciousness that surrounds us … like an open bowl maybe. If you start being curious about bowls you'll find that image everywhere!

Life, time, stories go in circles and circles inside circles. There is the whole story, the flow, the narrative, and then there are the small happenings, epiphanies, spots of time, often unrecognised beginnings and endings, the stories inside the story.

We won't understand incarnation until we set ourselves free from images of lines, maps and life plans. We can't explain or make a set of rules, a guide, for spirituality. We can only live. Think about the Nicodemus story (John 3:1–21) and the difference between a static faith, obeying a set of rules, and a way of seeing, living and loving. Nicodemus asks for direction but 'the wind blows where it wills'. What he needs is insight. Not how to believe, not creeds or dogmas that try to place an absolute meaning at the centre of life, but how to live … how to be human … a language true to his experience of life, his own story to live by.

Life is made up of strangely sweet threshold moments when, like Martha (in John 11), we recognise something we have always known, or like Eliot are back where we started, knowing the place for the first time. There are messy edges, tensions, shifts of vision, uncertainties. The threshold is not necessarily a comfortable place to be …… but it is a place of angels.

Liturgy of the wind

The words the wind blows away …
conversations on hills
by the sea.

The trees change colour
as their leaves move
with the air
like a draught
that blows
between the lines.

The rainbow windmill
in the child's hand
is a wind poem.

You can hold the kite's string
but you can't capture the wind.

Sky-wandering larks
rise on the wind
like words
invisibly mending
the earth's hurts

and I remember
the first time I heard
my Swedish friend reading
a poem in her own language.

Mapping or dreaming

The oystercatcher's cry
is a rumour
we don't understand
and never will

while the corncrake mocks
from a place in the grass
we think we know
but never find.

These things live without
our knowing their meaning.
They have little need
of our seeking
and will, it seems,
always find us.

Easter 1995

(For Catherine)

A blown egg – decorated
with the blue of the darkest night
and a filigree of white; flowers
for a wedding, or a funeral.

You handled it with care,
trusted its endurance,
carried it, in your rucksack,
from an Easter tree
in Prague
across a continent
home.

Then like a risk
and a promise
you offered
into my hands
a way to think
fragility.

From the bridge

(Sunday, 6th October, 2002* – Dorchester on Thames)

In this *Wind in the Willows* place
the teasels along the river's edge
are made golden, as if for Christmas,
by the last light of evening
and a white horse appears
out of the shadows,
like a unicorn.

The evening seems to be offered
as bounty to the dead
in the same way as memory
holds my mother's gold brooches
that are long gone.

Light and approaching dark
dapple things with my thoughts
of all that is
and all that couldn't be.

So long afterwards
the storybook picture remains
without meaning beyond celebration
of the earth for the living.

* My mother died in February 2002. 6th October was her birthday.

The green chapel

(Summer 1995 – for Jan)

We have crossed a threshold
from a surface of summer heat
into a deeper consciousness.

A sea swell of moss and fern
rises on solid walls of rock
to the right and left of us.

Gently we honour this green
promised land, disturbed
by our kinship
with moist vegetation.

The Japanese Bridge at Giverny

(Monet, 1922)

An artist asks a question:
Do you dare
to cross the bridge?
This is a painterly question
suggesting that
on the other side
is the life I want to live,
on the other side
is a world livelier
than I am prepared
to admit.

Dreams are the greater poets
and poems will start
this side. The bridge
is the uncertain way.
It crosses over water
flowing into the shadows,
a constant shift
of light and colour,
the only distance
the paint offers …

Bowl

(Kiln Opening, Mulchelney, 17th September, 2005)

'Walk with it for a while,'
the potter said.
'Make friends with it.'

Its simple rounded form,
warm from the kiln,
fits perfectly
into my open hands.

I cherish its fragility
and delight in its modesty.
I am overwhelmed by such greatness
in detail: an almost forgotten oneness
with all that is.
I smell the earth in it.

There are others like it
but I know this one
will travel with me.
This chosen one
has soul.

I hold it like a monk
with a begging bowl
and look into its emptiness
waiting to see
what the day offers.

Sheepfolds

I love the shape of the fold:
the bowl-like roundness of stones
moulded one into another,
holding fast. Each one pulls
into the whole
each one bears witness
to the memory
of human and animal.
Andy Goldsworthy, I think,
is some sort of shepherd.

Stones together intensify space
quietly: enfold a holy emptiness:
space for imagination
and children's play,
ground for circles, cycles, curves,
ends that are always beginnings.

The story tells of a shepherd
who made his body a door.*
We still love the shape
of the words
that keep us safe
and bring us home.

John 10:6–9

Explorers not mapmakers

(Meditation on the story of the Transfiguration,
Luke 9:28–32)

How good it is that we are here.
This is It. We have arrived.
We will put up tents,
shelters, chapels, churches …
Others coming to this place
will see what we think we know.
Why move on?
We have found Identity and Meaning.
We will hold on to this experience
for dear life and human sanity.

But there is no holding on.
The cloud is upon us.
We are covered in shadow
and immobile in fear.
Risen and free, he dances ahead
and we must let go.
What we attempt to contain
within our poverty of understanding
is here no longer.
We leave behind one mystery
to follow another mystery –

a continual exploration
which allows no settlement
in the safety of the known.
No pitching of tents,
or making of shelters,
to protect our visions.

One who goes before
moves with all speed,
leaving as we arrive;
showing us that discipleship
is and always will be
the ever-new, ever-changing search
for what we have always known.

Ring of Brodgar (Orkney)

Are they calendar, clock or altar?
is a perfectly suspended question.
The wind whispers around them:
'here now, here now'
and they own their silence,
hold their peace.
They know the place
just right.

Theirs is a stillness
deeply rooted in story,
and the years
of being here,
sharing space
with grass and stars,
visiting painted ladies,
and sometimes rainbows.

Solentiname Resurrection*

I stand outside the frame
of this painting;
at the edge
of the garden, absorbing
promises of abundant life
intercepted by the shadows
of a graveyard of lost causes.

A ship on the horizon
offers the possibility
of sailing away, forgetting
…… or maybe wondering forever
about secret echoes of Eden,
and the scent of golden apples.

But the emphasised eyes
of a colourful stranger
won't let me go.
They urge me
to live fully
in the outbursting
here and now.

This is no dreamlike meeting
with a comforting Jesus,
no wandering in and out of story

but an everyday, any day encounter
with a disturbing image.
It might be
on a mountain, or in a High Street

in a painting or in a garden:
that's the immediacy,
the wonder, the fear
the challenge ......
and there's no easy escape –
the ship sailed
long ago.

* This poem was inspired by Resurrection, a painting by Olivia Silva, one of the Solentiname poets. In the 1970s the Christian-Marxist priest Ernesto Cardenel set up an artists' commune on the island of Solentiname. The community became increasingly involved in Nicaragua's liberation struggle. Resurrection appears on the back cover of The Peasant Poets of Solentiname, translated by Peter Wright and published by Katabasis, London, in 1991.

The dovecote at Woodwick House*

How long ago did the doves fly?:
long enough for a path to be made
through buttercups, cow parsley
and a few bluebells, beside the river
down to the sea.

How long ago did the doves fly?:
long enough for leaves to grow
over and in, hiding the door,
and the earth to reclaim
stones carefully chosen
by long-ago builders.

How long ago did the doves fly?:
long enough for the dust to gather
on the makeshift altar,
the candle to go out
and a poem to be written.

How long ago did the doves fly?
Maybe just before the key turns
the door creaks open
and I wait beneath
garlands of green,
unable to name the loss.

* At Evie, Orkney. The dovecote is in the gardens of Woodwick House and is now used as a peace chapel.

In Regent's Park

(28th September, 2006,
For Margaret with love)

Summer's last roses
bloom late this year
and their petals blow
strange patterns across
the path of coming winter.

Shall we think that somewhere
in this weary world
old women are getting up
at dawn each day to queue
for bread to feed the children?

Shall we look for words
to grow old in, poetry
for the grief of the world

or shall we be extravagant
with the morning, pause
to smell the roses,
let the language
of scent and colour,
the hush of friendship,
be enough for today?

A sort of creed for a wet day

I believe in
the rain running off rooftops
waterproofs, umbrellas,
the wild rose petals
and the creased leaves
of lady's mantle
where a few drops stay
like diamonds in the sun.

I believe in
the smell of the moist earth,
mushrooms, rotting wood, drenched leaves,
like yeast, bread dough,
death.

I believe in
the sound of water over rocks,
waves on the shore;
in the possibility of stones
turning into sand,
on the way to becoming
nothing.

Words in the sand

(John 8:1–11)

Here we go again
dragging her out, voiceless,
into the heat of the crowd,
into the unforgiving light
of our probing minds.

We are as impenetrable
as the desert stones;
unaware that we use
a nameless woman's body

to show a method
for working with groups,
or dealing with anger;

a way to embody
his forgiveness.

Yet what has she done
except to live imperfectly
her given, sun-kissed life

and by choice or no choice,
chance or mischance,
to love, as many do,
unwisely and too well.

His head is bowed.
The sun and her nearness
warm his back.
When he looks up
the lustre of her eyes
takes him by surprise.

He blinks and bends again;
writes in the sand
the words of a poem
harder to read
than the method
we seek to learn.

Happening

A death dark sky;
a night sexual
with plant and leaf
and the movement of a fox
his eyes, bright on us,
caught for a moment
in the car's intrusive headlights.
He turns, melting
into the damp-floored wood
with purpose beyond
our lives, yet mingled
with our being,
lifting the moment.

Palimpsest

It almost ceases to be
a gravestone

and becomes a secret
garden, a memorial
to hiddenness.

Rain runs down
in runnels like rivers
through a many-coloured land
of strange trees.
Water is carving
its own story,
making another layer
of meaning
over writing
we can no longer see.

Gate to the Isles

(On a painting by Winifred Nicholson)

I like the promise of thresholds:
gates, doors, bridges, arches,
like rainbows,
beckoning places
where the colours
are all expectation;
where insights wait
to be given;
where a voice
might be found.

I have learnt to trust
the edges; feel the wonder
of becoming;
live in the bursting moment;
neither bud nor flower,
chrysalis nor butterfly,
here nor there
but the way through
to the store place
of impressions –
a sea-filled
morning place.

At the hospital

A woman parks her car
and goes into the hospital.
She walks along corridors,
past rooms full of people
she doesn't know,
past lifts going somewhere
important.

She arrives at a room
marked 'Radiotherapy'.
She is taken inside
by a nurse
who does this all day.

The woman takes off her clothes
and puts on a white gown.
She doesn't speak.

She is taken further in
to a room of machines
with a high table.

She takes off the gown
and lies on the table.
She closes her eyes
and thinks of flowers.

But today the machine
refuses to work.

A repair man comes.
He wears blue overalls
and whistles 'Amazing Grace'.
He carries a toolbox
like the one she has
at home.

The man greets the woman
with a wave and 'Hello, Love.'

The woman is asked to lie still
to avoid disturbing the machine.

No-one seems to notice her body
with no clothes on.

The man mends the machine.
The machine attempts to heal
the woman.

She dresses, goes to the car
and gets in.

The end of summer

Her dolls' picnic
lies neglected
under the bee-loud veronica.

She dawdles
down the cracked concrete path
her hands cupped
around an offering
of steaming tea.

At the greenhouse door
smells draw her in
like a familiar blanket
on a too-hot night:
tomatoes,
spicy – like cinnamon perhaps,
cucumbers,
light and grassy,
hardly scented at all,
the musk
of the chrysanthemums
he's grooming for autumn
awaiting their crowns
of blowsy blooms
her mother hates,

sweat, a hint
of peppermint.

He unfolds the chair,
plants it in the earth

and sits waiting for her
like the Sunday school image
of God she will reject
when she becomes a woman.

Plants dangle their red and green fruits –
Christmas tree baubles
she mustn't touch.

He offers her a ripe tomato
but she's already looking away
to her mother's face
at the kitchen window.

She runs back to the house
with nothing in her hands.

Refugees

A place like a pause,
an interruption, where seeds
lay, undying.

The air is light and empty,
the cottage long gone
in the process,
of building and razing
communities.

Poppies and marigolds,
way of life and death plants
emerge, like a conversation
I've never had
yet might hold
in my open hands.

What Peter knew ...

(Acts 3)

What energy did he tap
that day at the Gate
called Beautiful?
Something deep within himself
reflected in a beggar's eyes;
something treasured in his heart
since that first healing day
when Jesus said, 'Tell no-one.'

Sick, lame and demon-possessed;
broken bodies, smelling of suffering:
they had all come,
searching out the one
whose looking was love,
whose touch could liberate
body and mind.

All day Peter followed
into the place of unknowing
where imagination
ran riot – his own confusion
a first step
to healing.

Sometimes he knew
the holiness
of ordinary moments
fully lived.

Other times
the knowing
and the unknowing
were like a fever

in his own home:
a chance setting
for a miracle
and a wordless way
of learning.

There,
Jesus took a nameless
woman's hand
and attended
to her need
and her longing.

So she could take
her own next step
and rise again
to welcome all the marvel
and messiness of human life
waiting, always waiting
at her door.

All are in need
of healing, Peter knew
as he looked with love
into the eyes of one man

that day at the Gate
called Beautiful
and saw himself: a man walking
not on water,
which he quickly understood
is not an element
for walking …
but step
by creative step
on the good earth.
That was freedom,
that was the miracle –
knowing the element
for which he was designed.

Part Three:

Because of Love

Introduction

Love is an over-used, often misused word. I know that by using it here I run the risk of moving into sentimentality, but I think the risk worth taking because the word 'sentimental' is often used disparagingly for what is written about ordinary day-to-day living, home, homemaking and motherhood. Home, however small or large the scale of our thinking, is an image of limitless potency.

Love is the dance of life, the inherent rhythm, in the work of makers and bakers, carers and cleaners … potters and gardeners … What we do is not easily detached from what we feel. It's no accident that in the resurrection story Mary thinks at first that Jesus is the gardener.

So what *happens* because of love? We look into the face of a stranger or friend and discover something that goes beyond crowded café or empty hillside, beyond time and place. We may sit at the bedside of someone seriously ill, perhaps not praying exactly but noticing things around us with a strangely heightened awareness. We may be deeply moved by the words and lives of people unseen. This love with mindfulness is, I feel, the essence of spirituality and prayer: being alongside, in knowing or unknowing those who suffer or rejoice, reaching out to others and making their sickness, anguish, hunger, nakedness … or joy our own.

Because of love, stories are told, seeds sown, saved and shared. Because of love we *do* something apparently useless: light a candle, perhaps, and in some small way our being and seeing is transformed. We are giving out of what we do not have for there is no endless supply of love within us. It comes as we give it.

We begin to see through the eyes of love: we begin to look with open eyes, see with open hearts; to trust the human self, to know something of what it is to be alive, to *see how things are* and *how they could be*. Seeing, attending, imagining lead to transformation which is not improvement, moral or otherwise, but deep connecting and healing.

This is the down-to-earth intelligence of the heart, which moves everyday things into a wider arena. It reconnects reason and emotion while being always aware that the heart has 'reasons' way beyond what we can explain. Sometimes the urge to make sense is destructive. Love is a vision that challenges logic and reason as the highest forms of functioning. Perhaps ultimately our deepest desire is to relate to and be at peace with others and the earth, our home.

Love is what we leave behind and what we take with us. Love will survive.

Prayer

I think of mossy stones
settled in the sun:
the ruins of a cottage:
once a place to hold off the cold,
huddle by the hearth fire
and feel safe in;

I think how the heart
breaks open
and a seed rests
where once was fire,
roots itself like a memory
then bursts out –
seeming to touch
everything.

Naming

(John 20:16)

There are the many words:
enough to tell the story

and there is a way
of saying a name.

When Mary heard her name
in the garden in the first light
of morning
the word took flight
and tinted ordinary things
with butterfly colours
as memorable
as the shaft of light
coming in through the church door
on Easter Day.

Because of the way
he spoke her name.
Because she knew it was safe
in his mouth.

How things are

All the way home
that autumn day
he talked about leaves.
He had watched
them come down,
picked up one or two,
looked at them sadly:
'The trees are broken …' he said
and tried to put the leaves back
on the lower branches
just within his reach.

'No,' we said, 'they don't fit back.
The tree will sleep now. In spring
the leaves will come again.'

Beginnings of a smile …
then he ran among the fallen leaves,
enjoying the sound,
learning how things
are meant to be.

An April day – a few clouds
in a blue sky,
a hint of warmth
in the air, softness
and the feeling
that something new
is just beginning.

William, glad to be out,
looks up at the trees,
sees the first signs
of leaves and cries out:
'The spring did it!'

Strawberry gateau

A crowded city street
and a hand on another's shoulder;
the man in the collar turns
to face fully the other's despair.
He knows him:
'What can I do?'
'I need food.'

The café is crowded.
The man in the collar
moves his companion
towards nourishment:
cheese, meat, soup,
healthy, wholemeal bread.

The other is not to be led
so easily; a spark of life
shows briefly in his eyes.
He speaks slowly, thoughtfully,
'What I really want …
is strawberry gateau …'

thick and wet with pleasures
long untouched:
strawberry lips, moist buttery cream,
green meadows, a summer breeze

and dreams of a land
flowing with milk and honey.

Magician

(Marc Chagall)

Does he have rainbows
in his head,
colours to orchestrate
festively, to pull out
like silk scarves
from a hat,
to create a world circus
and process it
across canvas after canvas?
He is ringmaster
and clown, making merry
with a fabulous yellow cow,
and a little tree,
all blossom.

All nature's funny side
he cares for
with transforming energy.
He looks at everything
from everywhere,
saying: *I have flown here*
to live and love –
a gesture of celebration.

We might glimpse a night
of remembered heat
a midsummer orgasm
with an outburst of flowers.
Painterly messengers
travel between worlds
looking for the way
to live all the colours
of a wanted life.

Soapbox

My box of plain wood
gives nothing away.
It stands firmly on the floor
with its lid closed.

I open the lid,
lift out handfuls
of ready-to-use words,
close the lid
and stand on the box.

From this height
it's easy to use the words
to exclaim, proclaim,
assert, discuss,
without creating conversation.

When the words are used up
and I'm feeling vaguely dissatisfied,
I try opening the box again.
There's not much to see.

I reach into the dark space.
The words are more difficult
to get hold of now:
hands, tongue, lips, voice,
legs, skin, hair, arms,
eyelashes, eyes, fingertips:
a touch, a look, a kiss.

They shape themselves
into two bodies fitting well
together.
I feel warm inside
and wonder at the power
of words.

The box is almost empty now
but when I put my hands deep
into the darkness at the bottom
I discover three more words
hidden in a corner, easy to miss.
They are worn from use
but when I speak them
they shine like new
I love you

The candle we light ...

is more than itself.

It's a flame of many memories:
a lifetime of relationship:
lover, partner, husband, wife,
brother, sister, parent, child.

It's the fragile flicker of chance
that makes encounters
into friendships.

It's the touch of a lover,
the smile of a neighbour,
a child who puts a hand in mine
silently telling me
there is tomorrow
and all will be well.

It's a drench of fresh rain,
a garden of sunflowers,
impish daisies
that come from nowhere,
a good meal,
a cat to stroke,
a cup of clear water,
the last rays of the setting sun.

Where cure is impossible;
it's healing and peace.
It's closeness in loneliness,
comfort in mourning,
love to share.

It's a farewell

to the one who has died
and a yes of breath to the living.

It's the ripeness and wholeness
of all beginnings and endings.

We light the candle
to let go shattered dreams
and all that might have been

into the dark space,
into the greater hope.

This moment of shining
in a tiny bit of the darkness
is prayer and blessing.

It will burn itself out
but never die.

I do not know what resurrection is
but I believe it comes quietly
in moments of light
where love is strong
to bear regrets
and banish fears.
And for now
that is enough.

Carols by candlelight

An unknown baby's cry
in the church tonight
is a sound for all
who see the shadow
at the heart
of the candle's flame.

We can pretend no ease
on the way to being human.
It's always surprising
but rarely without crying.
Even the cushioned words
of our carols can't muffle
the sound of crying
or the sharp edge
of Herod's sword.

A rumour of Christmas

Is this the moment
when a birth and a promise
put out the brash lights
let in the rumour:
a whisper, a faint flicker,
a murmur of angels singing
for shepherds and war-worn travellers,
kings and troubled bishops,
Mary, and all women
who, in the bleakness of winter,
worship with a kiss?

Wedding song

As if the beautiful future
is here in the joyful now
dance, dance
for this wedding day,
swing, swing
in the rhythm of life
that follows the one
who makes the pure water
flow like honey-sweet wine
the gift of hope,
the best for last.

Follow the one
with a sackful of wings
to lift us off our feet
in starburst
colourburst
flowerburst.

Today is the world's beginning
Today every word
turns to poetry
Today is our dancing day.

Beginnings

We have come unclothed
to the land of no limits,
where moisture,
like damp earth,
is warm and welcoming.

Here we may drink
at deep springs,
feel freely;
wander untroubled
among delights
which embody any god
I seek to know.

The language here
is smiling and weeping,
touching and listening.
What is shared
understands
we are all virgin
somewhere.

Blue beans

(For Robert and Alison)

The welcome is sensitive,
warm with understanding.
Here is many-scented hospitality,
free moving of thought and feeling,
a growing place where I am glad to be.

In this space
the art of caring is natural
as carefully chosen pictures
and pure soft bed linen.

Nurtured plants come up
with beanstalk speed
and might surprise me one day
with a magical crop of blue beans.
This is exactly how things are –
organic, oddly coloured
and promising
that all shall be well.

Emmaus

(Luke 24:13–32,
For Sheila)

Outside the locked doors*
on the long walk away
from death and despair

something happens.

In the tenderness of the evening
a fire deep inside is rekindled
and tired limbs are warmed to life.
The darkening sky is strangely near
and the breath of a breeze on the skin
is a remembered voice:
a whisper of scripture:
'Did I not say it must be like this?'

Later, around the table of home,
the empty space
becomes a place
to trust the unknown.
Bread breaks and eyes open wide
to a light full of stories:
all things gathered
in loving and sharing.

See John 20:19

Olive tree

(December 2005, for Jan, in Palestine)

You tell me of dry earth and sand,
of olives oozing oil
in your pockets,
and the way the story of the land
is deeply carved
into its ancient trees.

I think ever since I first heard
of Gethsemane and suffering
I have known of the olive
as a tree of many gifts and signs.

So today I'm moved to tears by this one
potted and out of place
beside a blow-up Father Christmas
on a dull December day
at a Garden Centre
in England.

An ordinary miracle

(For Christopher on St Andrew's Day, 2000)

The first to come out of the crowd
as the sun goes down:
a small guardian of the future
with trust in his eyes
and hope in his hands.

In him, Andrew sees something
of himself; meets a memory:
a shadow of long ago when he was a boy,
his energy unsullied and his vision clear;
a whisper from the depths of his being
about fairness and sharing
and simple answers.

A disciple in an impossible position,
reminded of his first care –
to feed others –
wondering about miracles;
a boy bearing food, risking ridicule;
here, now, late in the day
they make their way
to one whose work
is in such small but costly acts;
who sees in each hungry face
an essential fragility,
a childlike joy
not wholly lost
to a bigger future.

And so …
in this once upon a time moment …
the story begins.
Outrageous hope, outspoken love
are released like nudging angels
amongst people longing
for comfort and community,
sensing the beginnings of friendships.

Child, disciple and the one who understands
just and equal sharing:
know there will be enough
to go round,
refuse to say, 'It can't be done.'

So it happens – the great feast:
hearts and hands, baskets and pockets,
open,
neighbour gives bread
and peace to neighbour,
each makes a place for another
and in this most ordinary of miracles
all are fed.

Sheela-na-gig at Kilvickeon*

We might easily miss it:
high on the east wall.

Some say it's a warning about lust
but I like to think it mouths a 'yes'
to birth and beginnings.

There's no evil here –
the devil, they say, can't stand
the sight of a woman's sex.

This is a place of storied light,
where angel questions
hang in the air;
a layered place
where we might hear
in the silence,
the intimate murmurs
of the unremembered
who lie deeper
than the marked graves.

A story is being told
in language just beyond
our reach.
So don't use the word 'god' –
or even 'goddess',
unless you hear
the rumour.

A sheela-na-gig is a carving of a woman with exposed and sometimes exaggerated genitalia, found on religious buildings. Kilvickeon is a ruined 13th-century chapel and burial ground, near Scoor on the Ross of Mull.

Rosary

(Glasgow, April 2002)

The plane comes down to the city
on this grey April day.
There's rain in the air.

The random colours
I wondered about
take shape as piles of rubbish.
I think of my beads from Ghana
made by compressing plastic bags,
loo seats, boxes, bowls …

and how throwaway colours
hold the potential
for transformation: touch
each bead of imagination
with endless possibilities.

The garden

In the beginning is a garden
and an almost warm wind
with a promise
beyond dead of winter.

A path wanders through a litany
of labelled plants:
Glacier, Winter Sun, Midwinter Fire.
They hold the light with care,
so that sunlight leaps
like Lenten Fire
from side to side:
from buff, to bare yellow,
from warm pink to brilliant orange.
This is not a preparation
but a coming through

to the shape of a poem.
The garden is fertile
with metaphors. The fragility
of flowers offers understanding
of ourselves and our desires.
Our feet feel the rhythm
the grip and push of March.

I wonder how to think the presence
of plants – what language to use
for a garden filled with fragrance
of daffodils and somewhere beyond
memory the exotic scent of pomegranates.

In the hollow winter hand
of whatever we might call god
these few strangely sweet hours
in a particular place
might hold all things.

Who saw us come into the garden?
Who sees us leave
or knows we were there?

Skara Brae*

An inquisitive wind
lifts a blanket of sand
and uncovers secrets
whispered 5000 years ago
in the shadows of a gallery
of great stone circles.

Sun and sea, wind and rain
now touch again
innocent patterns
of survival and sharing.
Here is home ground, common ground;
midden-warmed – a good place
for people to be.
Compost of themselves
 – no waste but sign and identity;
an earthy protection,
a binding together
in community:
here is our place.
Out there is the whole world.

My eyes are drawn
to the makings of story
without war or weapons:
a dresser at home's centre
to celebrate sacred daily living.

The shelves are empty –
nothing to attach a poem to,
except rumours of peace
and echoes of attention
to little things:
bone beads, pins, pendants
and paint pots;

not nuggets of truth –
but parables of earthiness
to warm the singing stones.

The community of Skara Brae, on the Bay of Skaill, Orkney, existed before the Egyptian pyramids were built and flourished many centuries before construction began at Stonehenge. Skara Brae is special for many reasons, but particularly because the community's ways of resolving conflict appear to have been peaceful – no weapons were found at the site. The later village was build into, and protected by, a midden: the domestic rubbish heap. The people of Skara Brae were better at both living in community and recycling than we are!

Sir, you have no bucket ... and the well is deep

(John 4:11)

The clanking sound of an empty bucket
echoes like an elaborate theory
that makes devastating sense.

But what makes the sad world lovely
is that somewhere it hides a wellspring
without a bucket.

We may never find the well
but our thirst will be satisfied
by the search, the coming close
and wondering:
does the one know
and the other feel
or are the knowing
and the feeling
together in the flow
that carries the pain
and the joy of the world.

Weep over injustice,
rejoice in goodness,
love outrageously.

Let uncertainty
flow on the stillness
of our bodies
and the story be told
in freshly drawn water.

This poem looks at our attempt and desire to hold life within elaborate theories/theologies which are often devastating to wholeness. Whereas embodied thinking means we can't detach ourselves from how what we do, or decide, feels – for us and others. We carry the pain of the world on our bodies (what the whole Jesus story is about surely?). If you separate mind and body you can rationalise any atrocity.

John 4:11 is one of my favourite Bible verses. I feel that the woman at the well story shows us a lot about accompaniment, giving out of what we do not have, and the flowing together of heart and mind.

Part Four:

A Soaring Vision

Introduction

I recognise – most people do – those moments when life surprises, when you look into the face of another human being with understanding that goes beyond time, place and words, when the heart leaps and vision widens – soars almost. Annunciation, that angel-nudging that makes us *see*, and incarnation – the expression of our full humanity in relationship, that which is deepest in us and all things – are inseparable.

This sort of vision isn't about hurrying to a receding future but turning aside to see ordinary people as they are, valuing everyday life for what it is: a fragile miracle we have in our keeping!

I think of Mother Julian's vision as she looked at the hazelnut in her palm: a little fragile thing that is all that is made and exists now and forever because of love. I think of the women of India who have formed seed co-ops to treasure and share seeds. 'Hold the seed in your hand, sister' is their now and forever love story.

When Mary anoints Jesus's feet with precious oil (John 12:1–8) we can see this ordinary act as moving beyond the personal. This story is more important personally, socially, politically than we sometimes think and its imagery is often misused. It's an act of love, defined by a soaring vision which is carried to a suffering world. Mary's apparently foolish act is laughing at the facts of the world, not letting them have the last word. She is living her dream.

Image becomes imagination. I see a myth as a story of an action or event that becomes universal, for always. So where do myths begin: in great works of heroism *or* in the beauty and wonder of quietly repeated everyday acts of love and loving that, like Mary's, gather light, resist evil, lift abused humanity, let thinking soar … and we hear the music of dailiness above the customary voices of history?

Mary

(John 12:1–8)

At his adored and human feet
she pours out the essence
of her story
in sweet-scented unction
which mingles for ever
with the soft womanliness
of her free flowing hair.

No cold duty to distant majesty
could initiate this act of grace.
Her body holds the fire
of luxurious loving.
Her release
is moist and sweet,
as it runs free for him,
and a suffering world
to which she will carry
the soaring vision
that defines her love.

Unease

Not disease exactly
but like it:
a sense of something
wrong
that looms and grows
and closes in
like a dark cloud;

a sense of air
not fit for breathing,
of weird light,
the distance hidden
in a brown haze,
the sun looking too bright,
feeling too hot;

the knowledge that people die
unheeded, untended,
from weather, hunger
and the ways of men;

that children cry and few hear,
rivers dry up, trees die
or are destroyed.

While all the time
a market force,
an invisible army,
of abstracts

marches on triumphantly,
taking over market*places*

where once people met,
told stories, shared news,
where once there were clowns
and jugglers, and laughter;

marches on, conquering communities
and destroying dreams.

And through the people's tears
one prayer remains
and that the best:
'Teach us
to outgrow our madness.' *

* *Originally the words of the Japanese writer Kenzaburo Oe, quoted by Nadine Gordimer in* Living in Hope and History: Notes from Our Century, *Bloomsbury, 1999, London, p.94.*

'Hold the seed in your hand, sister'

In Bhatinda in Punjab
even the trees have stopped
bearing fruit because the bees
and butterflies have gone.

The wells are dry in Rajasthan
where thirsty cash crops
grown for export
drink all the water.

Bathua, amaranth, mustard
the people's wholesome greens
won't grow alongside wheat
sprayed with herbicide.

The peasants' life-supporting fields
rich with pulses, millets, paddy
have become plantations
full of bananas
for the rich world.

37 varieties of wheat
and thousands of strains of rice
developed over the centuries
are being stolen by seed companies.

Farmers lured to buy
hybrid cotton seeds, white gold,
to make them millionaires,
kill themselves with pesticides
they can't afford.

The knowledge of the people
is being converted into the property
of global corporations.

Multinational companies
with a perverted view of the earth
see bees as thieves
stealing pollen.

While in the Himalayas
in terraced fields the women tend
a rainbow wonder of food:
Jhangora, Marsha,
Tur, Urad,
Gahat, Soya beans,
Bhat*

and women in Bengal grow
150 varieties of greens.

Women all over the world
nurture and exchange seeds
set up seed banks:

maintain self-reliance
and biodiversity.

Who will feed the world?

Those we still call poor:
eat what the women grow,
live in housing
made from natural materials,

make what they wear,
don't consume the commodities
of the Market,
the junk of food companies,

those who live simply,
work with nature,
make rice artworks
to feed ants and birds,

live forgotten, unseen, unpaid
by the men of power,

those who know
that inside every seed
lies a story world
that can't be bought,

those who understand abundance
based on sharing:

they will feed the world.

Jhangora: Barnyard millet; Marsha: Amaranth; Tur: Pigeon pea; Urad: Black gram; Gahat: Horse gram; Bhat: Glycine soya

If you would like to know more about seed sovereignty: read the work of Vandana Shiva or explore www.navdanya.org

A wing and a song

We can't ignore the birds –
or miss the miracle that raises
them beyond earth's pain.

They circle above
our devastated dreams,
a challenge to fanciful imagery:
that green hill far away
and the stark beauty of three crosses
against the reassuring blue
of a sheltering sky.

Beauty has grown sick
with the weight of paradise.
Neither the scent of spring flowers
nor a cleansing wind
from the distant sea
will cover the stink
of death.

It clings to clothes,
seeps into flesh,
offends the nostrils
of the righteous.

Yet this festering mound
is life to some

celebrated in the sound
of people's voices
lifting their abused humanity,
singing the people's story
singing to live
tomorrow.*

And the wing-tips of the birds
write resurrection on the sky.

In her book Journeys through Song, *Maggie Hamilton tells the story of the people of the Visayan Islands, who sing love songs on a rubbish dump.*

Gipsy Lane

Silence is restless
in this story place

a simple line
on the landscape
between here and there,
an ancient right
of small way
connecting communities;
not to be lost
yet still to be found.

I know the place:
a stile here;
a familiar tree root there:
'This one looks
like an elephant's foot.'

Caravans paused
at the edge of the path.
People lived here
for a while;
cooked, ate and slept
between birch and towering beech;
woke in the morning
to carpets of bluebells,
primroses, violets,
stitchwort or startling red campion.

The green spread
of dog's mercury
still hints at something
beyond our knowing.

Children have grown,
the people and their homes
have moved on

yet I hear them still
above the chorus
of murmuring trees:
gypsy voices, barking dogs,
the crackle of fires,
and footsteps,
always the footsteps,
marking the path
home.

Moon eclipse

(3rd/4th March, 2007)

There are scars on the surface
of all our distant dreams
and we see no place
of our belonging.
The shadow of our days
on earth, how the shadow
haunts us.

Before

First foot in the night fields
before dawn and the rising sun,
the air still sweet
in the time before birth
and beginnings.

First foot in the night fields,
trusting the brush
of each moist blade of grass,
the vegetable scent
of each carefully placed step,
the touch of moth wings,
the rhythm of stones
under invisible feet.

First foot in the night fields,
unsure, waiting for the light,
loving the waiting.

Advent

In these low sun days
light is a small place
to be alive in,
a space for stories,
music around fires,
candles lit
for the dying.

Enough
to keep hope alive; to know
how small things make a world:
    lanterns that swing in the wind,
    a frosty moon,
    glimmer of starlight,
    fairy lights,
    a lamp at a window,
    headlights and porch lights,
    a twinkling tree.

We are the light-gatherers,
collecting our uncertain secrets
and keeping them

like golden chrysanthemum heads
carried late from greenhouse to house.

To understand a little light:
that, and waiting
for the first daffodil
to yellow the world.

Snowdrops

(For Fred and Anthea)

The churchyard is cold.
Beneath dark branches
the ground yields little.
This coming isn't easy.

A white presence –
milkflowers,
milk of human kindness –
is beginning to push through.

They are the colour
of whispers,
before the babble
of daffodils,
showing, like arctic fields,
a little green
for remembering.

When Adam and Eve
left the garden, it's said,
they were comforted
by an angel
who turned snowflakes
into snowdrops.

Lanterns to guide
the way to the dance.

But now just a touch,
the hint of another story,
something murmuring underground
– a rumour of spring.

Taking the stone home

(For John)

A coracle carrying Columba,
a man hoping to be a saint,
reaches a shore
strewn with pebbles
touched by the rhythm
of the moon.

Sea-washed feet
might once have walked
on the stone I hold.
It's warm, if a warm thing
is what I need;
cool when I want shadows.

Its ancient presence
bears the story
of our common humanity,

holds regrets and remorse
as a burden to be thrown
far out to sea –
a symbolic act
of pilgrims.

And yet its colours
in the sunlight
would seem to be a sign
of grace to lighten
the moment –
the way grieving is carried
alongside joy.
This is something
not to be missed:
as dependable
as the stone in my hand
is unlike any other.

Corncrake

(Matthew 6:33)

Nutty noise-maker,
most enigmatic of birds,

almost a name
for the unfound
and unseen,

for points of reference
that keep moving about.

You could watch the field
all day and never see it.

There is only that sound
like an angel's laugh
telling us
we're always close
never there.

The potter

He offers into the fire
a possibility shaped
in earth and water.

And in time takes out
and holds in open hands
a form getting closer
to his holy grail.

One hundred times one

(Rembrandt's Self-portraits)

Steady eyes,
no pose but a penetrating
gaze into the human heart.
He tries out
quest, affirmation,
plea or cry.
Tests each emotional state:
paints prayers, thoughts,
meditations,
uses the wonder of light
to reach the centre
of his regret
and ecstasy
in small parts:
hair and hats,
a look in the eyes,
a piece of armour,
a left hand,
a wrinkle of skin.
This wholly new way
with light harmonises
substance and shadow,
makes all things
possible – even endurance
of pain.

He looks for dreams
paints them, maybe,
paints and paints.
But never quite realises
the vision
until, in the end,
there is only
his own face
looking out
through the laughter
of Zeuxis.*

* Zeuxis was a Greek painter of the late fifth century BCE who sought the Perfect Form in the Platonic sense. He was praised in antiquity for his subtle use of shaded colour and faithful representations. Self-portrait as Zeuxis is one of Rembrandt's many self-portraits.

Listener

Wait in the space behind the words
of the child in a woman's body.

Wait with an open heart.
Be sensitive and patient

for the memory
may be only half retrieved,
the quiet not easy
to break

and the words
not necessarily
what you expect.

Once they are spoken
don't try to hold them
or mould them
to your own understanding.

Let the story be;
free the storyteller
to laugh and let go

and her laughter
will be the sound
of resurrection.

Angels

There have been moments
when I could hear the love-song
of angels as they bend
a little nearer the earth.

And there is this moment
when one skinny child
unconstrained
by the Abbey's stony majesty
clasps his unlit candle
and waits for the flame
to be passed.
His expectant face
is enough to light
the world.

Light

Our days of summer sun
are milled into flour,
sweetened and disturbed into honey,
amazed into the sight
of a late dandelion.

While deep in the dark
wheat grains wait
wanting light.

At one with the waiting,
we dream a harvest field
as November sun burnishes
the spent gold
of beech leaves.

Light the Advent candles
but know the flower head
of flame
you see today
you'll never see again.
Don't imagine you can hold
the secret of the
burning bush.

New Year snowdrops
against the dark earth
are a transfiguration
of words
into winter air:
a kind of light
for all time.

From the Abbey's high windows
light floods the shadows:
a blessing and a beckoning.
Outside it washes
like a smile
over stones, sea
and wide horizons.

The *Night Path*
that Andy Goldsworthy created
from broken chalk
takes you on a lonely walk
guided by the light under your feet
and the moon beyond.

Huge light of the sun
is a ball of hot bubbling gases
millions of times bigger than the Earth.

See how the sunflowers
in their yellow veils
turn their heads
in worship.

Helios.
Hyperion.
The sun may be God.

Olafur Eliasson's *Sun** was indoors,
embodying the question:
is there any building or word
big enough to hold light
when even the smallest glimmer
says it all?

* *Huge indoor sun exhibited at Tate Modern in 2003.*

Being

I look for words
to capture the moment
between something
and nothing:

the raindrop shadows
on a dead leaf,

a cloud
across the sun

and its dark shape
on a distant hillside
just before the heat
dries it out,

the movement of air
that puts out the candle flame
and carries kites
high over our heads,

the exact, never to be repeated,
movement of muscles
and formation of lines
that is a smile.

Where angels watch ...

Churchyard, Kempsford

Not a graveyard where only dead people
and mourners come but a living place
where a boy hides amongst headstones
bigger than him, weaves in and out
of tree trunks and tall grasses;
runs into the sunlight
living his story.
He knows the place,
stops and looks:

'Here's the seat, Grandma.'

At St David's

William, aged two, looks up,
then runs to the steps
of the font.
He sits
not making a sound.
Like David, water-drinking saint,
asleep in his tomb,
he watches and waits,

knows the place.
Whatever happens elsewhere
in past or future
a quiet form of history
is being made – now –
in this given moment
at the water place.
Drink it deeply.

Light-gatherers

Those who know their part
in the intricate pattern of being;

those who are attentive to the whole
and the particular and hear
what lies on the other side
of silence;

those who desire justice
with all their being;

those who push out the boundaries
of the possible and re-dream
the world;

the standers and the starers
the lookers and the seers;

those who give unexpected gifts
and share their ice cream;

the makers and the minders
the helpers and the healers;

the seed savers and seed sharers
the bread makers and bread breakers;

those whose imaginings
breathe life into failing spirits
and bring hope in troubled times;

those who discern what is good,
discover what is hidden,
dance to life's rhythm,
in poetry and song;

those who make love
and trust their longing for life;

those who live simply and gently
alongside all living things;

those who do not miss
the ray of sun
on a little flower;

those who forgive,
those who accept forgiveness;

those whose stories show
    the value of our struggle,
those whose stories help us
    understand who we are
    and find our souls,
those whose stories dance us
    into life;

those who live with uncertainty
and the deep hard secret of love;

those whose laughter shows us:
    mercy, friendliness and solidarity,
    that there is more than logic and reason,
    that the facts of the world
    are not the end of the matter,
    that there are many truths
    none of which need defending
    with violence,
    that stories of suffering
    don't have the last word;

those who see angels,
who hear the people's crying
and feel the earth's pain;

those whose random kindness
makes life beautiful;

those who have thoughts
that could change their lives
and the lives of others
and go on doing so
for ever;

those who have low expectations
and high hopes;

those who sing Magnificat
and, like Mary, set out with joy
into wide and unknown futures.

Elemental

When my time is over
and fire has consumed
all flesh, take my dust
and scatter it
where you can feel
earth, water, rushing air
that I may be
whole.

Then take away with you
memories, burning in fire,
fresh as air, rolling as the sea,
still as the earth
and this shall be
my resurrection.

Surprise

Dandelions on dung heaps;
daisies in stone walls;
the long goodwill
of the damp-floored forest
where old leaves
nurture new trees
and the hopeful energy
of creativity's seedbed
nourishes the silent outrage
of spring;

these chip away at petrified logic
and play with reason's straightjacket;
outgrow the private;

make me face my own name
as if it belongs
somewhere else;

make me lose myself
in the huge surprise of life
in the jack-in-the-box,
head-over-heels world
of multi-coloured movement
that outbursts
the first
and every
'I love you'

Apples

I have a sort of dream
of a hidden orchard and the soft air
of a late summer evening.
Butterflies feast on fallen fruit.

In the fading light, I reach up
and hold an apple
in my hand.
It rests there
against the stars
just visible
through the branches.

I smell its sharp-sweet flesh,
sense its mystery.

I'm holding life and legends
in one hand.

Apples were there at the beginning
before words,
before they took their place
in story.

Inside this red-gold globe
are tiny storehouses for the heady scent
of orchards in full bloom
and the flowering of human dreams.

Once monks were buried in orchards.
Imagine a graveyard in blossom time.
How could you not believe
in resurrection?

An Afterthought ......
The Seven Colours of Imagination

Iona rainbow

The rainbow
arching the Abbey now
is like a thin air bridge
between the stones on the shore
and eternity
with no meaning
but poetry.

Red

is the smell
of strawberries
on a summer evening

and warm earth
beneath bare feet.

Reaching out red
is the unsettling sound
of a song of longing.

Red is wind on the hill
and the hot blast
of a trumpet.

Like peppers and pimentos,
it's the colour of fire
and warning: be careful
you might get burnt.

Red is the stop and look
powdered pigment of Anish Kapoor,
Wassily Kandinsky's radiant brush strokes,
Chagall's angel and one of Franz Marc's horses:
the lively one (the quiet one is blue)
and Andy Goldsworthy's poppy petals
wrapped round a hazel branch.

Ochres from the earth
run blood red when wet
and madder is the rhythm
of the rubia tree roots.

Red is raw; red is birth.
Red is spilt blood.

Disturbed earth bleeds poppies.

Red I think
might be the colour of God.

Orange

You bring a gift
of clementines – almost
from Palestine
where, you tell,
2000 years of care
for land and ancient trees
brings a plentiful harvest.

We sing and cry and dance and laugh
the glowing orange warmth
of hope

and warning:
eye-catching orange paints
dangerous parts of machinery.

'Orange,' Kandinsky said,
'is like a man convinced
of his own powers'

or a woman maybe
with a basket of fruit
in Drury Lane.

Brian Keenan was persuaded
by the colour orange
that he would survive.

The robes of Buddhist monks
glow in orange contrast
to the plain wooden bowls
in their hands.

Orange is the settled background
of Winifred Nicholson's
Honeysuckle and Sweetpeas

and something disturbing
in Van Gogh's sunflowers.

It's the lump
in the end of a stocking
on Christmas morning,

the smell of luxury,
a reminder of poverty.

Orange is the varnish
Stradivari used,
the sound of a violin
playing in the rain

and a bunch of marigolds
on an unmarked grave.

Yellow

is the silent yes
of a field full of buttercups
and the sound of a harp playing
in the first warmth of the morning.

It's the feel of dry grass
on bare ankles,
brimstone butterflies against sky blue
and a garden loud with bees,
the smell of haymaking
and a field of wheat grain waiting.

Yellow is the colour of kindness,
amber, honey, saffron,
the oily taste of sunflower seeds,
eggs, butter, Easter morning
and how the blackbird's beak
resists the dark.

It's the glowing beard
of Chagall's *Jew in Green*
and the elm leaves
that Andy Goldsworthy
laid over a rock
at low water in Dumfriesshire.

Yellow is fear, jaundice
and blisters on tired feet;
old documents, letters,
and newspapers
at the bottom of a drawer;

sand through an hourglass
and over-wintered apples.

It's chrysanthemums laid on a coffin,
and a light in a distant window.

Green

is the earth's holding
of river, pond and lake,
the way the hills roll
towards the water,
a many-shaded landscape.

It's tenderness and generosity
lavish, yet spreading itself lightly
with something saved
for tomorrow.

Green is a child's first words,
the side of the apple
that isn't blushing
and the sea where it isn't blue.

Green sounds like a rippling river,
and soft wind in the trees,

smells like the wet grass
on a spring morning.

It's peppermint ice cream,
the woodpecker's back,
the gloss on a mallard

and Georgia O'Keeffe's
vibrant oak leaves.

Green is the colour my mother wears
in a black-and-white photograph.

It's the other side of the fence,
jealousy, envy, pus, infection,
the colour eggs go,
and a bruise as it heals.

Green is bendy and pliable,
what I want to hold on to
in old age.

I think the other side of death
might be green.

Blue

is a Hebridean sky
many-blued, clouds shadowed
almost purple, ready to weep
for the colour
of an artist's longing.

The bluest of blues
comes from beyond
the seas
Renoir took it to celebrate
La Parisienne
and Titian
the purity of the Virgin's robes.

The distant blue
is childhood's remembered hills,
my blue heaven.

Seen from space
the Earth is blue

and underfoot
the colour will fade
with the dying
bluebells.

Gentians that grow
on a famine road
can't be told,
the colour won't hold.

It's a story handwritten
in washable ink.

Indigo

is the Hebridean sea, around rocks,
where it isn't turquoise.
It's the deep skies
of a Jolomo painting.

Louis Marcoussis used indigo
to make the space beyond
the open door, and the rhythm
of the background sea.

Indigo is the glowing polish
of aubergines and the shine
of Renoir's wet umbrellas.

It's inky writing,
a once upon a time story
from over the seas,
and the exotic usurper
of home-grown woad.

Indigo is a dark memory
of starving peasants
in Bengal and Bihar
forced out of food growing

to make the colour
of a bruise, a tragedy,
threatening clouds
in a summer sky.

Violet

is a shadow colour,
the opposite of light
complementing yellow.

A mourning colour
'Sad and ailing,' Kandinsky said

but Monet saw
fresh air as violet.

I wonder, did he sense
ultraviolet light?

Christopher Wood sought
a perfect shade of violet
to show the depth
of the sea's mystery.

While Winifred Nicholson's *Two Agapanthus*
have a lightly violet touch
which is also a far away longing
in *Blue Mountain Flowers*.

Violet is silky and secretive,
blushing damson dark
amongst the late summer leaves.

Violet is the deep purple
of Cleopatra's sails*,

beloved of songbirds and honeybees
yet hardly noticed.

It's the last colour
on the rainbow spectrum,
ending the known,
beginning the unknown,
calling to something beyond itself –

something between the rainbow
and its enigmatic echo.

* Antony and Cleopatra, *William Shakespeare, II.2*

Notes and acknowledgements

'Mary' was first published in *A Telling Place: Reflections on stories of women in the Bible*, Joy Mead, Wild Goose Publications, 2002. 'Surprise' first appeared in *Connect*. Earlier versions of 'Well-being', 'Carols by Candlelight', 'Skara Brae' and 'Taking the stone home' first appeared in *Coracle*, the magazine of the Iona Community. 'A rumour of Christmas' first appeared in *Hay & Stardust: Resources for Christmas to Candlemas*, Ruth Burgess, Wild Goose Publications, 2005. 'An ordinary miracle' first appeared in *Holy Ground: Liturgies and worship resources for an engaged spirituality*, Neil Paynter and Helen Boothroyd, Wild Goose Publications, 2005. 'Easter 1995' was first published in *Making Peace in Practice and Poetry*, Joy Mead, Wild Goose Publications, 2004. 'Elemental' first appeared in *This Is the Day: Readings and meditations from the Iona Community*, Neil Paynter, Wild Goose Publications, 2002.

Photographs © Joy Mead. 'Moon eclipse' photo © Andrew Mead.

I greatly appreciate Sophie Hacker's encouragement and support and particularly her permission to use her painting *Little Flower* on the front cover.

I am grateful to Grevel Lindop for permission to use 'The seven colours of imagination' as the title of the last section of the book. The words are taken from number XI of 'Twenty-One Poems for Wood Engravings by Thomas Bewick' by Grevel Lindop, included in *Selected Poems*, Carcanet, Manchester, 2000.

The poem which opens this book is dedicated to Donald Eadie, whose words at a gathering long ago in High Wycombe inspired the thinking behind the poem, and whose friendship is an unfailing support and encouragement to me.

As always, a big thank you to everyone at Wild Goose Publications for their dedication, understanding and sheer hard work. I am especially grateful to Neil for his unwavering care, patience and attention to detail.

Also from Joy Mead

A Telling Place (Wild Goose Publications)

Reflections on stories of women in the Bible

In the story of the encounter between Jesus and a Samaritan woman at Jacob's Well, the woman gives him a drink and he talks with her. It is a sensitive story of meeting, giving and receiving – a telling place. All sorts of things happen around water: creative, celebratory, promising things. Joy Mead imagines the women mentioned in the Bible as central to their own stories, rather than appearing briefly on the margins of a narrative which reflects a world perceived and led by men. Her meditations on these women express her belief that their stories are not just about 'women`s issues', but are relevant to both men and women. They explore an incarnational theology, earthed in creation and the possibility of transformation, and a perspective on society centred on mutuality and relationship. This is a book not of certainties and answers but of explorations and questions. Just like the interaction at the well of Jesus and the Samaritan woman, or Jacob and Rachel, it is about looking into the puzzling heart of all things and being enriched by the experience.

ISBN 978 1 901557688

The One Loaf (Wild Goose Publications)

An everyday celebration

A book which explores the making and the mystery of bread – growing, making, baking, sharing – in story and recipe, poetry and prayer. In bread we see the true connectedness of all life – the uniting of body and soul, spirit and material. It is not just a symbol of life, it is life itself. Without food, life is impossible, so eating becomes sacred. Take and eat means take and live; to share food is to share our life. Jesus, in a simple act, made eating and sharing sacred. This beautiful illustrated book helps us to love the 'dailiness' of bread, the holiness of eating and the justice of sharing.

ISBN 978 1 901557 381

Order from www.ionabooks.com

Making Peace in Practice and Poetry (Wild Goose Publications)

Joy Mead presents five practical workshops, for groups or individuals, to explore the use of words and poetry in everyday life. Unique among the species, humans create their world through language and imagination. In this we have the potential to be aggressive, violent and oppressive, or gentle, creative and vulnerable. Words express and shape what we are or might become. We are all poets when we attempt to express the essence of our own experiences. As we tell and listen, we develop our sense of community and our humanity. Because the personal is also political, this process creates peace between people, in society, and among nations.

The readings and activities in this book aim to lead us to a deeper understanding of how we use language. As we become more discriminating in our use of words, so we can better tell our own stories and relate to the experiences of others.

ISBN 978 1 901557 848

The Iona Community is:

An ecumenical movement of men and women from different walks of life and different traditions in the Christian church. Committed to the gospel of Jesus Christ, and to following where that leads, even into the unknown. Engaged together, and with people of goodwill across the world, in acting, reflecting and praying for justice, peace and the integrity of creation. Convinced that the inclusive community we seek must be embodied in the community we practise

Together with our staff, we are responsible for:

Our islands residential centres of Iona Abbey, the MacLeod Centre on Iona, and Camas Adventure Centre on the Ross of Mull

and in Glasgow:

The administration of the Community
Our work with young people
Our publishing house, Wild Goose Publications
Our association in the revitalising of worship with the Wild Goose Resource Group

The Iona Community was founded in Glasgow in 1938 by George MacLeod, minister, visionary and prophetic witness for peace, in the context of the poverty and despair of the Depression. Its original task of rebuilding the monastic ruins of Iona Abbey became a sign of hopeful rebuilding of community in Scotland and beyond. Today, we are about 250 Members, mostly in Britain, and 1500 Associate Members, with 1400 Friends worldwide.

Together and apart, 'we follow the light we have, and pray for more light'.

For information on the Iona Community contact:
The Iona Community, Fourth Floor, Savoy House, 140 Sauchiehall Street,
Glasgow G2 3DH, UK. Phone: 0141 332 6343
e-mail: admin@iona.org.uk; web: www.iona.org.uk

For enquiries about visiting Iona, please contact:
Iona Abbey, Isle of Iona, Argyll PA76 6SN, UK. Phone: 01681 700404
e-mail: ionacomm@iona.org.uk

Wild Goose Publications, the publishing house of the Iona Community established in the Celtic Christian tradition of Saint Columba, produces books, CDs and digital downloads on:

- holistic spirituality
- social justice
- political and peace issues
- healing
- innovative approaches to worship
- song in worship, including the work of the Wild Goose Resource Group
- material for meditation and reflection

For more information, please contact us at:

Wild Goose Publications
Fourth Floor, Savoy House
140 Sauchiehall Street,
Glasgow G2 3DH, UK

Tel. +44 (0)141 332 6292
Fax +44 (0)141 332 1090
e-mail: admin@ionabooks.com

or visit our website at
www.ionabooks.com
for details of all our products and online sales